Talented And Gifted Program
Institute for Learning & Teaching
University of Massachusetts Boston

Sonnets from the Puerto Rican

D0868905

Sonnets from the Puerto Rican

Jack Agüeros

Hanging Loose Press
Brooklyn, New York

Published by Hanging Loose Press, 231 Wyckoff Street, Brooklyn,
New York 11217. All rights reserved.
No part of this book may be reproduced without the publisher's
written permission except for brief quotations in critical articles.

Printed in the United States of America
10 9 8 7 6 5 4 3 2 1

Cover photography by Katherine McGlynn.
Cover design by Caroline Drabik

Hanging Loose Press thanks the Literature Programs of the New
York State Council on the Arts and the National Endowment for the
Arts for assistance in publication of this book.

Acknowledgments: *Agni, Boston Review, Brujula/Compass, Callaloo,
Hanging Loose, The Massachusetts Review, The Progressive* and *Parnassus*.
Some poems appeared in the earlier book, *Correspondence Between the
Stonehaulers*.

Library of Congress Cataloging-in-Publication Data

Agüeros, Jack
        Sonnets from the Puerto Rican / Jack Agüeros.
            p.   cm.
        ISBN 1-882413-22-9 (pbk.)
        1. Puerto Rican–New York (N.Y.)–Poetry. 2. Sonnets, American.
    I. Title.
    PS 3551.G845S66   1996
    811'.54–dc20   95-49711
                                                        CIP

Produced at The Print Center, Inc., 225 Varick St.,
New York, NY 10014, a non-profit facility for liter-
ary and arts-related publications. (212) 206-8465

Landscapes

Sonnet for 1950   13
Sonnet after Columbus, I   14
Sonnet: Waiting in Tompkins Square Park   15
Sonnet for the #6   16
Sonnet for Heaven Below   17
Sonnet for Mars   18
Sonnet for Chuggers and Speeders   19
Sonnet for One Hot Summer   20
Sonnet: News from the World, Tompkins Square Park,
     & the Metropolitan Transit Authority   21
Sonnet: Tompkins Square Park, October 18, 1989, 5:45pm   22
Sonnet for a Mural at Arden House, I   23
Sonnet for a Mural at Arden House, II   24
Sonnet for Saturday, October 6, 1990   25
Sonnet: The History of Puerto Rico   26
Sonnet after Columbus, II   27
Sonnet for the Bicycle Rider's Leg   28
Sonnet on the Location of Hell   29
Sonnet for a Thousand Points of Light   30
Sonnet: The Face of War   31
Sonnet for Paradise Missed   32

Five Sonnets for the Happy Land Social Club Fire

   I. Sonnet for an Incendiary Affair: Julio Loves Lydia   33
  II. Sonnet for the 87 Dead Dancers   34
 III. Sonnet for Landlords, Lawyers, Judges,
           and the Courtroom Game   35
  IV. Sonnet for the Only Monument Around,
           October 1994   36
   V. Sonnet for the Orphaned Children   37

Sonnets for the Four Horsemen of the Apocalypse:
Long Time Among Us

   I. Sonnet for the Elegant Rider   38
  II. Sonnet for You, Familiar Famine   39
 III. Sonnet for Red-Horsed War   40
  IV. Sonnet for Ambiguous Captivity   41

Headlines from America, Banana Republic, Spring 1995   42
Sonnet for Naomi Who Asked Me   43
Sonnet for Chicago's Second Fire, July 1995   44

Love ...

Sonnet for My Heart in the River Below   47
Sonnet for the Censor   48
Sonnet for Love, the Good Book   49
Sonnet for the Me Afraid of Love   50
Sonnet for Death the Second Perfection   51
Sonnet for Your Return   52
Sonnet for This Life Like Death   53
Sonnet for My Coffin Now   54
Sonnet for My Longed-for Infarction   55
Sonnet for My Heart's Failure   56
Sonnet for You, My Moon   57
Sonnet for Me, Your Orbiting Dog   58
Sonnet for a Child Who Calls   59
Sonnet for the Lovesick Sailor   60
Sonnet Because You Love Me Not   61
Sonnet for My Appetite Disorders   62
Sonnet for the Blackbird of Silence   63
Sonnet for My Pawned Heart   64
Sonnet for What Ails Me: My Lost Heart   65
Sonnet for Love's Only Exit   66
Sonnet for My Imprisoned Tears   67
Sonnet for Death the Welcome Trip   68
Sonnet for Death's Warm Hand   69
Sonnet for Eloping with Death   70
Sonnet for Death, Kind Aztec   71
Sonnet for You, Disguised in My Dream   72
Sonnet for You About Me   73
Sonnet for So Soon Missing Her   74
Sonnet for You, Songbird   75
Sonnet Explaining My Periodic Silences on the Phone   76

Portraits

Sonnet for Willie Classen, Middleweight   79
Sonnet for Angelo Monterosa   80
Sonnet for Henry Ramos   81
Sonnet for Maddog   82
Sonnet for Joe Stella   83
Sonnet for Eloy Blanco, Painter   84
Sonnet for García, Clothes Rack Pusher   85
Sonnet for Raymond Castro   86
Sonnet with Twice the Lines   87
Soneto para Manuel de Dios Unanue, Periodista   88
Sonnet for Jorge Soto, Painter   89
Sonnet for the Cowbell Clapper   90
Sonnet: Self-Portrait for Yolanda Rodríguez   91
Sonnet for Clemente Soto Vélez, Poet & Patriot   92
Sonnet: Portrait of What's Next   93
Sonnet: My Speech to Death   94
Sonnet: Portrait as a Dry Thespian   95
Sonnet for My Conspiring Tears   96
Sonnet Substantially like the Words of Fulano Rodríguez
     One Position Ahead of Me on the Unemployment Line   97
Sonnet: Portrait of Me, Biology Alone   98
Sonnet: Portrait as a Happy Masochist   99
Sonnet for Generous Death   100
Sonnet: Portrait: Who is That Man in the Mirror?   101
Sonnet: How Shall I Weep for the Dry-Eyed Me?   102
Sonnet for the Charlatan Time   103
Sonnet: Love & Death, I Am Grown   104
Sonnet for My Godmother   105
Sonnet for Carmen Agüeros Díaz, Seamstress   106
Sonnet for Alejandro Román, Remarkable Rider   107
Sonnet: How I Became a Moving Man   108
Sonnet for Delgado the Driver   109
Sonnet for Miss Beausoleil   110

DEDICATION

For Mrs. Finnegan, the teacher at Benjamin Franklin H.S.
in East Harlem who introduced me to my first sonnet

Shelley's "Ozymandias"

and with special thanks to

William Shakespeare, Elizabeth Barrett Browning,
e. e. cummings, and Edna St. Vincent Millay
for their tutoring.

Landscapes

Sonnet for 1950

All the kids came rumbling down the wood tenement
Shaky stairs, sneakers slapping against the worn
Tin tread edges, downhall came Pepo, Chino, Cojo,
Curly bursting from the door like shells exploding
Singing "I'm a Rican Doodle Dandy" and "What shall
We be today, Doctors or Junkies, Soldiers or Winos?"

Pepo put a milk crate on a Spanish Harlem johnny pump
And drops opened like paratroopers carrying war news.

Then Urban Renewal attacked the pump, cleared the slums
Blamed Puerto Rico and dispersed the Spics, blasting
Them into the Army or Anywhere Avenue in the Bronx.

And nobody, but nobody, came back from that summer.

Just as Korea was death in service to the warring Nation
The Bronx was death in service to the negligent Nation

Sonnet after Columbus, I

We watched the stiff starched sails, the cotton and wood
On the scale of little boy boats blow onto our shore:
Our burned out tree canoes were larger and sleeker
The Caribbean was quiet, tranquil as ourselves, but

These men were all more hellish than any hurricane,
And nothing good came after, government after government,
English, Dutch, Spanish, Yankee, twisting the tongue,
Jail some, buy some, scare some, dope some, kill plenty.

Do you know the names of the ones in jail or why?

Sailed in our bays and put paper feet on our throats,
Paperhands in our pockets, papered the trees and land
Papered our eyes, and we still wait wondering when.

As for the names of the incarcerated? You and me.
Charge? Not throwing tea in the bay.

Sonnet: Waiting in Tompkins Square Park

My father used to tell me about the Great Depression.
Long lines of men waiting in anticipation of soup.
Long lines of men waiting in anticipation of interviews.
Long lines of men; waiting; in anticipation; waiting.

What I do now is wonder as I see long lines of men
Waiting for food in Tompkins Square Park, and women
Cast about the landscape of benches, boxes, tottering
Tents, transient as leaves blown by the wind off Avenue B,

And long lines of bodies sleeping on the park bandshell
Neatly distributed in rows on the stage like cards in
Solitaire, or a supine chorus line choreographed for a
Busby Berkeley film routine. This show my father never saw.

Or did my father see and censor, never mention to a child
That government was the Four Horsemen of the Apocalypse.

Sonnet for the # 6

The subways are full of smoke and acrid mists today. In this
Heat the haze is thick glass that turns everything upside down.

Thor is banging on the third rail, his sparks shoot down the
Newspaper birds flying in flocks in the dark. Vulcan's forge
Bellowing, coughing gas, ozone and foul fumes travelling faster
Than Mercury or Huracan or the express. Marijuana flavors
The smoke, and incense burned by Afro-American Muslims. What

Thoughtless God gave man drugs I wonder, when I see the old sign
With the Ordinance which Prohibits Cigarette Smoking, but the new
Generation smokes grass and only reads color video, and disobedient
Prometheus is to blame for fire anyway. Down here, like at Styx,
I am angry at the Gods, but at Hunt's Point a Latin lady gets on

And I recognize Quetzalcoatl, beak and plumes, and the train elevates
like a magic carpet over the Bronx to Pelham or Parnassus.

Sonnet for Heaven Below

No, it wasn't Macondo, and it wasn't Calcutta in time past.
But subway magic turned the tunnels into Beautyrest mattresses
And plenty of God's children started sleeping there. Some
Were actually angels fatigued from long hours and no pay.

This is an aside, but I have to alert you. Angels run
Around, don't shave or bathe, acid rain fractures their
Feathers, and french fries and Coca-Cola corrupt
The color of their skin and make them sing hoarsely.
The gossamer shoes so perfect for kicking clouds
Stain and tear on the concrete and in the hard light
Of the city they start to look like abandoned barges
Foundering in the cancerous waters of the Gowanus Canal.

Shabby gossamer shoes always arouse the derision of smart New
    Yorkers,
Mercifully, angels aren't tourists so they are spared total disdain.

Sonnet for Mars

Mars. I loved you once as much as I now grieve.
I envied your two moons, red planet. But now I see
Red blood, the color of armaments rusting and
Buried nuclear waste erupting, corroding the soil.

Face ripped by mining, face tracked by trenches
Blew open the ozone, cannons shredded the leaves
Hydrogen fire boiling the water to meagre icecaps
Impotent warrior, cannot make mists or spit clouds.

Mars. Where is the poet's song to the simultaneous
Eclipses of Phobos and Deimos, the painting with
The anemic greens of your last sterile spring?

Mighty warrior parched. Mighty warrior breathless.

Mars.
Now I understand the meaning of your desolate face.

Sonnet for Chuggers and Speeders

Everybody had been drinking wine and stealing beer
And opening hydrants and rolling grass and sniffing
Coke and heroin from capsules, pipes, paper shovels,
And sometimes shortened straws or glass pipettes.

The summer was one very loud radio and busting
Mailboxes. Winter meant the hospital in Kentucky
Except for the overdosed dead, and who, looking
In the mirror, who, we asked ourselves, were they?

And now I know that time is a train on a long closed
Loop, whereas death and disorder ride a bicycle built
For two with flame-forged chromium handlebars, plush
Sheepwool seat, ten-speed gearbox, but no brakes.

The train lumbers through predictable stations.
The desperate prefer to ride with exciting death.

Sonnet for One Hot Summer

This was a time for children and play, but hysterical
Helicopters darted through the black spreading smoke
Of violent fires like the canefield after harvest —
These ignited by bottles full of grief and gasoline.

A window went out like a Roman candle showering green
Glass. Running feet with scuffed shoes scrambled
The shards as if they were fragments of a history
No one wanted to recite, read, assemble or resolve.

Quique said, "Arriba the cockfight! I love the bantam,
Yet my silver goes on the one with steel spurs."
When the sirens played the official battle song
The people's chorus answered with bongos and bricks

But the angry oratorio was silenced by bullets
And the final score was: Natives nothing.

Sonnet: News from the World, Tompkins Square Park, & the Metropolitan Transit Authority

November, 1989. Japan owns two bricks more than half of
Rockefeller Center; Germany, Poland and Czechoslovakia
Are rising, smoke in China has risen over Tienanmen Square,
El Salvador is smoking, and Castro has given up tobacco.

On the home front, mergers and acquisitions are down,
The captains of Wall Street are laying people off by the
Thousands, New York elected a lawyer mayor who doesn't know
About taxes, stock transactions and conflict of interest.

The subway fare will go up and people will be arrested
For sleeping in, on, or near the trains, or stations
And a judge judged that it's constitutional to alchemize
Single room occupancy into conspicuous condominiums.

The homeless in Tompkins Square Park will take refuge
In *The News*. Ah, Capitalism! the three-card monte master.

Sonnet: Tompkins Square Park,
October 18, 1989, 5:45 pm

It could be a painting by Norman Rockwell or any American romantic
Landscapist: Old trees undress in the waning light and bleached
Leaves fall limp like soft garments at their feet. My weak eyes
Are about to say wood smoke hangs pretty, but my nose interrupts
Calling it acrid air. I squint creating a close-up, and then I
See the small figures from Pieter Breughel and Heironymus Bosch
In a field of shacks and cardboard co-ops in Gothic bloom as if
In a garden grown by Edgar Allan Poe. Old oil drums are recycled
Into open ovens with moist wood crackling, cooking and heating,
Serving as hearths to homeless men and women whose shadows mock
Them dancing and darting in runic time, randomly choreographed
By high spitting flames, and Hell is the name I now give this
Tableau, where the American axiom of abundance is annulled and
The quality of compassion has been left out in the rain, rusting.

Sonnet for a Mural at Arden House, I

From a Mural at Arden House:

> *"I have no words*
> *My voice is in my sword."*

Too bad, bold warriors, you left your swords behind
Speaking steel for you all these interim dead years
Bayard, Tamerlaine, Leonidas, Alexander, and
You too David, and you too, Indian Guatemozin.

We put the fierce in jails now, or hand them
Men to bleed as armies. Anonymous and gloryless
As clouds they march in dreary lockstep toward
Their fate, neither to win nor lose. And worse

Without a poet to sing their bloody names as someone
Has for you, converting doubtful deeds to flying
Lines that moved this painter to portray you in repose
Guatemozin, David, Alexander, Leonidas, Tamerlaine, Bayard.

You neither frighten nor inspire me now except in this:
I have a voice in words, and you are without swords.

Arden House is the former mansion and estate of the Harriman family
donated to Columbia University and used as a conference center.

Sonnet for a Mural at Arden House, II

From a Mural at Arden House:

She openeth her mouth   *Give her of the fruit of her hands*
With wisdom and in her   *And let her own works*
Tongue is the law of kindness   *Praise her in the gate*

Pocahontas only, with her breast exposed, attracts
Me now. She is the only dark one of the many
Classic beauties here arrayed in mythic dress
Enclosed by woods and topped by idealized quotations.
Pocahontas only seems to fit the common set
Of fact and fictions which we revere as history.

Cornelia has eyes too vague for Caesar's loyal wife
Beatrice too dull to fire the depth of Dante's mind
Judith too wan to wield the sword she lightly holds
Sheba too blue-eyed for a queen of Mesopotamia
Jeanne d'Arc no forecast no flicker of the final flames
Helen too faceless to be the force behind the fleet.

Antiquated male ideas have dressed you all in falsity
And only you attract me now, beautiful brown
Pocahontas

Sonnet for Saturday, October 6, 1990

Perplexing: Human beings rapidly piling up on streets
And sidewalks; vacant house windows silkscreened with
Fake flowers and blinds; common as leaves the fallen
Crack vials and the menacing eyedropper hypodermics.

On the wild west coast, adults killed time shooting
Each other from cars on the California freeways and
On New York corners anonymous drug peddlers hawked
Like junk bond brokers, and subways had sleeping cars.

The President acted decisively: arrested a colicky baby
Named Noriega; sent kids to play in the sands of Arabia;
Taxed beer; vetoed a civil rights bill. His son deftly
Plundered bucks in the savings and loan bank pillage.

Then I got it: Bush had declared America a Banana Republic,
And sealed the proclamation by closing the Statue of Liberty.

Sonnet: The History of Puerto Rico

Puerto Rico was created when the pumpkin on top of
The turtle burst and its teeming waters poured out
With all mankind and beastkind riding on the waves
Until the water drained leaving a tropical paradise.

Puerto Rico was stumbled on by lost vampires bearing
Crucifix in one hand, arquebus in the other, sucking
The veins of land and men, tossing the pulp into the
Compost heap which they used as the foundation for
Their fortifications and other vainglorious temples.

Puerto Rico was arrested just as it broke out of the
Spanish jail and, renamed a trusty, it was put in an
American cell. When the prisoner hollered, "Yankee, Go
Home," Puerto Rico was referred to the United Nations.

Puerto Rico, to get to paradise now, you have to ride blood.

Sonnet After Columbus, II

The bronze babies born on Borinquen sculpted three
Pointed stone dictionaries called "cemies" written in
Smells, words, symbols and pictographs we could not read,
So we rocked them babies and pulverized their culture.

Descended from this ignorance I sit savoring Puerto
Rican rum in October watching the sun rise over pointed
Mountains, see tri-pointed cotton clouds in the sky,
And tri-angular anger rises as I exhale hot cigar smoke
Puffing Indian Ritual, and blame me and Columbus and
Christians Arabs Africans avarice fat gold nuggets.

I wish the still-awake pregnant moon would fall into the
Sea birthing a diluvial tidal wave swamping the Santas,
Pintas, Niñas, Boeing 747's, dissolving time into new

Eyeglasses reading the world over with dogs that sing instead of bark.

Sonnet for the Bicycle Rider's Leg

There is a heart-stopping image stored in my memory that
Unannounced pops up like a jerky black-and-white movie
Of a man riding a bicycle with tireless rims on a high
Wire balancing a long pole, man on shoulders, everything.

But it's the zany bicycle messengers pumping madly on
Seventh Avenue who introduce me to the palpable meaning
Of old fashioned phrases like breakneck, death-defying,
Kamikaze, speed demon, zigzagging, and yes, hell-bent.

One in particular makes even those words seem weak and
New York cab drivers look like conservative turtles: He
Makes me freeze and my eyes glaze as he pedals by with
One whole left leg, but just the stump of a right thigh.

He casually snakes through the snarling traffic while I
Keep seeing his missing leg, and how he doesn't miss it.

Sonnet on the Location of Hell

You worry about hell: Where it is and what it looks
Like; how far you should go to safely peek at it;
What to do to avoid it; how to get others out of there.

Haven't you seen the sudden dumping of human beings
On all the streets and tunnels of our city? Don't they
Look like Jesus freshly deposed, twisted and limp like
Licorice in the lap and arms of His Holy Mother Mary?
Jesus was dead only momentarily, as these men and
Women are, but there are no holy arms eyes or mothers
To cry and cradle these dead until their resurrection.

We have made this grotesque Hell on Earth and burn the
Helpless with the silent flame of rust. Worriers, listen:

Neither God nor rabbits' feet can stamp these fires out
For Hell is our holy arms folded, our holy voice silent.

Sonnet for a Thousand Points of Light

People were accumulating on the streets and curbs like
Garbage waiting to be collected, but the landfills were
Full, sanitation trucks were busy in rich neighborhoods,
And public apathy was opportunely at an all-time high.

So, the Commissioners declared, "Sleeping in and around
Garbage cans is deceptive: Unless people can prove they
Are refuse, we will arrest them for converting stoops
To cabañas, subways to parlor cars, boxes to bedrooms,
And refusing our offers of recycling." The moral majority
Was silent, but two head-doctors spoke surprising us by
Saying, "Nuts or not, they are smart to stay out of our
Bellevues." When the new liberals were heard from at last
They happily chanted, "Let's house them on *your* block!"

Were these the thousand points of light I had been promised?

Sonnet: The Face of War

The face of war is your face. It is your face in the mirror
Wearing a sign that says, "I let them do it, I agreed with
My silence, voted for it with my passiveness, sent them my
Proxy endorsing it because I did not run into the streets
Screaming, 'Stop it now, this is not truth it's television.'"

To see the face of war, look in your mirror, not television.
It's your face casually donating your sons and my daughters,
Your face cheering Arabian sandbox games on the color screen.

War is your face supporting men who drink oil crude or sip it
Super-refined on the rocks out of barrels, or drunk, puke it
At sea, and still collect their premiums and profits. War is
Not fought with joy sticks like Nintendo or Super Mario and
The children who fall cannot kick, nor stand up ever again.

Face, pick your side: Your children or the oil oligarchy?

Sonnet for Paradise Missed

The Yankees kicked up the tropical grass and planted cement
after acres galore of bulldozing and rearranging the terrain
making it look like a Hollywood set. They bought land clear
down to the glorious ocean and just a toe before the salt
began, they built a swimming pool. They evicted the native
lizards and installed parrots that sang Muzak and broadcast
tapes that screeched "Welcome Friends" and other ingenious
phrases. Cleverly blocking the breezes with plate glass they
refrigerated the air, teaching the trade winds who was boss.
They did allow the sun to shine all day but at night they
gassed the dark with neon, embarrassing the shy fireflies.

When all was thoroughly falsified a new species bloomed that
furiously signed picture postcards of paradise missed and
said, "Wow, Puerto Rico is real cool, so where's the casino?"

Five Sonnets for the Happy Land
Social Club Fire*

I. Sonnet for an Incendiary Affair: Julio Loves Lydia

Julio, 36, loved Lydia, 45, in 1990. Lydia loved candles
crucifixes and Virgin Marys. Julio Gonzalez leapt from
Cuba to the Bronx but left his daughter. Lydia had 2 sons
and a granddaughter. Julio made lamps in a factory, when
laid off Julio washed cars, peddled on the streets. Lydia
worked nights at the Happy Land Social Club. Lydia loved
reggae and salsa, took coats, worked late to make $150.

Julio never argued, seldom drank. Julio told Lydia to
stop working at the club. Lydia said she couldn't. Julio
went to the Happy Land, downed several Cokes and found a
plan in his hand. Julio bought one buck's worth of gasoline,
filled a bottle — his jealousy fire bombed the Happy Land.

Julio quickly killed eighty-seven people all at once very dead.
Got 25 to life. Lydia escaped unburned. Julio still loves Lydia.

* In its time, the largest mass murder
  in American history, 25 March 1990

33

II. Sonnet for the 87 Dead Dancers

Under a torch in the harbor they worked hard days, nights
dreamt of sweet mañanas in Latin America or Puerto Rico.
Weekends were the Happy Land, where they poured alcohol on
tired feet, and massaged their souls with music until they
danced, neutralizing work days, bosses, weak coffee, short
pay. Spanish spoke them to them, and whirling to salsa or
body to body in boleros, the heart smiled, the spirit soared.

No one sang "Fire!" Swift flame and his slinky partner smoke
danced so fast all were fried in three-quarter time. Honduras,
named by Columbus and meaning depths, suffered most, lost 48
national treasures. They finally traveled airmail first
class, finally dressed in fine black bunting in the latest
wooden luggage; finally met the President of their republic.

But when he said "Welcome," rude death had sewn their mouths.

III. Sonnet for Landlords, Lawyers, Judges, and the Courtroom Game

Blind justice took over but it needed a seeing eye dog.
Murder became people vs. landlords. The lawyers mixed
the cards, said, "Pick the red-hot lease. Your bets now
please." Card one Jaffe, two Weiss, three DiLorenzo.

Rich Alex DiLorenzo had 200 buildings and a warrant
for his arrest for prior fire violations: no sprinklers,
no emergency lights, no assembly permits. Rich Jay Weiss
was married to a movie star and leased from DiLorenzo.
Weiss's *pana* Jaffe, sublet to Elías Colón, dead in the club.

Sucker Law flunked anatomy, math too: Landlords had no
hands to cuff, only wrists to slap. Paid peewee fines of
$210,000, no jail, just 50 hours of community service.

When the judge woke up, Hispanics were worth $2,414 each; 87
cadavers had been swindled; seen-it-all death shook his skull.

IV. Sonnet for the Only Monument Around, October 1994

The Happy Land still stands. Smoke stains the cornices
of its few small windows, hangs over the transom, like
bunting, of its only door. Offerings of flowers are sad
not because the plastic has faded and live leaves sered,
but how they show that the living poor cannot even keep
the dead since their life is strain enough. The PTA paid
for a sign; simple and dignified the 87 dead stand listed
in alphabetical order. They never stood so still in life.

A prayer is pinned to the spontaneous shrine: An anonymous
poet worked their names into a rhyme. Across the street a
city sign has elected officials announcing that a "granite
monument with the names of the dead" will rise in September 1994.

Under my October feet, a ditch full of debris is the only monument
around: It's dedicated to disrespect for Latinos, living or dead.

V. Sonnet for the Orphaned Children

I feel pensive and old like the cannon on top of the
round brick jail on Governors Island. A cold fall
morning hugs the harbor, subtly presaging winter to
come, and I wonder if I will live to see the City's
promised Honduran Cultural Center. Did DiLorenzo
ever correct his violations? Did Weiss and Jaffe
mend their grubby ways? Lydia, what do the Saints
say to your candles? Julio, what would you like
for an epitaph? Valladares, escaped DJ, do the 87
dead dancers haunt your hip-hops? Judge, will the
Spirit of Christmas Past visit your death bed?
City Fathers, where is the $210,000 you collected?

Orphaned children, will the monument ever be built,
will it read you a story, will it kiss you goodnight?

Sonnets for the Four Horsemen of the Apocalypse: Long Time Among Us

I. Sonnet for the Elegant Rider

The way I get it is, that when the world is about to end
Four horsemen will come thundering down from somewhere.

One will ride a red horse, and his name will be War.
One will ride a white horse and his name I don't get
since it's Captivity. Does that mean slavery? I don't
want to guess about these things, but translations can
be treacherous. One will ride a black horse and be named
Famine. I get that. Now here's another part that leaves
me scratching my head — one will ride a pale horse, and
since when is pale a color? He is named Death, and I
think this translator has him on the wrong horse. Death,
I know, rides the white horse, which symbolizes his purity.

You see, the future tense is wrong, since nothing is as now, or
as inevitable, or so personally elegant and apocalyptic as Death.

II. Sonnet for You, Familiar Famine

Nobody's waiting for any apocalypse to meet you, Famine!

We know you. There isn't a corner of our round world
where you don't politely accompany someone to bed each
night. In some families, you're the only one sitting
at the table when the dinner bell tolls. "He's not so
bad," say people who have plenty and easily tolerate you.
They argue that small portions are good for us, and
are just what we deserve. There's an activist side to
you, Famine. You've been known to bring down governments,
yet you never get any credit for your political reforms.

Don't make the mistake I used to make of thinking fat
people are immune to Famine. Famine has this other ugly
side. Famine knows that the more you eat the more you
long. That side bears his other frightening name, Emptiness.

III. Sonnet for Red-Horsed War

Obvious symbolism; let's call it blood-colored; admit
War jumped the gun on the apocalypse a long time ago.

Isn't it shy Peace that deserves free transportation?

What horse would Peace ride? Peace is usually put on a
Dove, but is so rare it ought to ride the extinct Dodo
of lost feathers we infer, and song we never heard.

War is vulgar, in your face, and favors harsh words.
Rides recklessly, and lately has even learned to fly;
drops pink mushrooms, enjoys ugly phrases like body
count and megacorpse. Generals love War, worship it by
sanctifying pentagons. When War shakes your hand, he
rips it from your arm; shoot and burn is his lullaby.

Like Kronos, War dines napkinless on his raw sons or
any burned flesh. Look, War is apocalypse all the time.

IV. Sonnet for Ambiguous Captivity

Captivity, I have taken your white horse. Punctilious
Death rides it better. Dubious, I try to look you in
your eye. Are you something like old-time slavery, or
are you like its clever cousin, colonialism? Are you
the same as "occupied," like when a bigger bird takes
over your nest, shits, and you still have to sweep? Or
when you struggle like the bottom fish snouting in the
deep cold water and the suck fish goes by scaled in his
neon colors, living off dividends, thinking banking is
work? Captivity, you look like Ireland and Puerto Rico!

Four horsemen of the apocalypse, why should anyone fear
your arrival, when you have already grown gray among us
too familiar and so contemptible? And you, Captivity, you

remind me of a working man who has to be his own horse.

Headlines from America, Banana Republic, Spring 1995

One percent of Americans own forty percent of the wealth.

Thirty percent of Americans have one hundred percent of the poverty and Government will soon deliver less to more. The minimum wage won't buy a burger, unemployment is rising and the workforce is downsized. Five million Americans are in jail or on probation. The South chains prisoners again and the State separates from Religion, killing wild Waco babies.

That's the news, here's the editorial: Christians, remember the Roman lions? Remember the Governor washing both hands? Remember those dictators stuffing closets with new shoes? Remember our Pentagon franchising Latin American torturers? Remember the name for countries with absent aristocracies, hungry babies, shoeless kids, agribusiness, landless peasants?

Banana Republic, exhume your revolutionary Declaration now!

Sonnet for Naomi Ayala Who Asked Me

Naomi asked me to write a poem about *sereno* but the
word means so much it could be the serene one; or
that side of night walking the city crying time and
announcing that all's well; or that side of night
dressed in see-through dew; that side of night a badly
parked cloud of humid oxygen; that side of night that
only visits Caribbean mountains; that side of night that
frightened our parents into old words to warn us like
paludismo and *pasmo,* ague, catarrh, and chilblain;
that side of night who makes you wonder if he is foe
or friend; that side of night whose hand is a crisp
lettuce you shake and greet familiarly forgetting his
Latin name. Naomi, *sereno* could be that side of night

flying like a wet kite, violining the starry skies.

Sonnet for Chicago's Second Fire, July 1995

Mrs. O'Leary's cow didn't kick the lantern this time.

"Hog butcher to the world," Sandburg said. Oh shame,
shame, pig-king city fathers, shame: 500 old people
trapped in their pens, squeals sealed by negligence!

Heat smashed in where fear had double-chained the door
and screwed the window tight. Poverty had hocked the
five-inch fan. No one warned "Be cool!" Heat placed his
flameless gloves on toothless mouths, passed corpses to
the city morgue. The chilly Coroner knew how to conduct
the dead to Potter's Field waving faceless inquests in
the air like notes to the Pied Piper's tough shit song.

Chicago! The slaughter passed 500! The Coroner hollered
for extra ice! The Burgher belched for his speech writer!

Chicago, shame, Billy Sunday *should* have closed you down!

The final count of the dead due to the heat wave exceeded 700!

Love …

Sonnet for My Heart in the River Below

The city is dressed in a gray sheet of November air
Chilled to forty-two Fahrenheit, considerably warmer
Than my heart, cold not due to the winds blustering
Over the bay, but because I think I have lost her.

Renovations and repairs on the Brooklyn Bridge have left
Only two benches. We sit. I discover warmth on her lips,
Heat in her shining eyes; her look and her smile are a
Woolen blanket that tucks in my little boy heart and

My hope soars higher than the stalagmites stretching
In all directions that populate the skyline here, but
Here on the gracious curve of this pioneering bridge
Where Roebling bethrothed two boroughs with filigree

Cables, I cannot create a love more complex, more tenderly suspended
Because she is gone, and my heart is an ice cube in the river below.

Sonnet for the Censor

Is this love or death I feel? Your fingers lightly
Press around my larynx. Not asphyxiating, but
Impeding my ability to mouth words for the simple

Ideas that, like petrogylphs with incised images around
A Taíno ballfield, line the periphery of my brain. But these
Stones have stills from the movie of our nights, and you
Crimp my description of the prototype instrument the
Universe uses to slice each month's first taste of moon.

I have already spoken of the machine that manufactures
Tiny comets. It is your black hair undulating that
Propels them into their accelerating parabola tracks
And it is your smile that ignites them with light.

Now I realize that to speak of love or death non-sequiturs
Alone will do: Squeeze more. Let go.

Sonnet for Love, the Good Book

Love is not anyone's child that can be scolded or made
To kneel silent in a corner; sent away early from the
Table because it speaks chewing, or be put to bed with
Toast and milk for being willful. And don't wait for
Father to get home, because Dad can't go to the street
And punch Love the tormentor in the nose for harassing
You. Love is not a question with sides weighable by a
Judge for equity or right and wrong, or a company sold
In preferred shares — ask any fool who ever said, "Love
Forever is mine alone." Love speaks out of turn in hard
Translations, and is like a good book borrowed: Read it
With great care and gusto since a bell may ring; it may
Escape from your custody and enter instant circulation.

Never say "This is my book," but "I am enjoying it now."

Sonnet for the Me Afraid of Love

I am a gamecock who close to triumph turned and raced
Letting tiny fear with no talent shrink my testicles,
Seize my heart, and with shorter talons slice my soul.
No mitotic starfish am I and thus can't regenerate a
Heart from the one shred left after my self-slaughter.

Now nothing seems as good as the neck-wringing a coward
Cock earns, but death sadistically avoids me and I live
On rich sighs while my life feels like a meatless soup.

What's left of my breath is beleaguered by your spirit:
Wherever I wander your shadow falls in step at my side.
Especially in my large darkness your absence glows red
And what others call silence I hear as your lyrical echo.

What made love look like a dragon in disguise when it's a
Baby that needs to be lifted, held and otherwise intuited?

Sonnet for Death the Second Perfection

The letter that I want to write is perfect: All i's are
dotted and t's are crossed, all p's and q's are minded
and no rules of grammar broke. My purpose is to win you
back, so my sentiments are linked like lace and I have
asked two courteous eagles to carry the thoughts that
weep in every open vowel and tangle amidst consonants.

Yet my hand is stiff as a rock, and I sit torpid like a
dumb buoy in the bay warning of shoals and shipwrecks
while only a wake or a scurrying wind can ring my bell
or make my lonely horn blow low or moan. My testicles
have gone to the size and color of rejectable prunes,
and I realize that I am dead, and it's too late for

Letters now. Knowing this, I gladly offer my open hand
To Death, who after your love is the second perfection.

Sonnet for Your Return

You took everything: Yourself. Left me sitting in the
empty box we once called home. It's true that I'm the
one who breached a solemn promise and thus no shadow
falls over you. No, I do not weep for furnishings or
goods, it's just that the solitude ate my whole song.

Love has harsh hands and raucous laughter: Harbors no
hesitations, redeems no uncertainties, forgives no less-
thans, dances in no margins. Yes, I was wrong, but are
you right surrounded by reluctance, and speaking with
the silence of trashed pride? I still hear the same song
I heard when I met you, and will. Remembering your smile
is nearly as rich as smelling you, and now in the nights

your voice blows into my dreams. These ghosts are my wealth,
fully populating the empty space where I dream till you return.

Sonnet for This Life Like Death

This life tastes more like saltless death. I love you
still but rejecting you I killed myself and turned into
an empty box which cannot resonate or sound even when
hard-banged. My nose turned to the lilies too late as

it had shut down. My eyes are skinny from overeating
their harsh diet of deep blue and any shade of gray. My
ears are wingless and can't even find echoes to nest in.
My heart lost its meter, and irregular beats embarrass
and redden the bugged eyes of my doctor's emotional
machines. I shaved my fingertips hoping to bring back
some sensations, but my mind plays only you, while my
deep-felt aria of love lies silent awaiting your baton.

How now can I deliver a heroic couplet to shatter glass
when six feet of your loss dam my lachrymals and larynx?

Sonnet for My Coffin Now

Open my coffin so I can jump in. It's better to lie there
with your memory than to be alive like now with my heart
full of rocks and my mind bleeding my love for you in a
red cascade. I have already packed my eyes with your smile
and when they close my lids no darkness will enter to crowd
my pupils or irritate my irises. I have dressed up in my
black suit of resignation that on earth I had the best in
you, and thus could have no more or finer reason to leave.

Open my coffin so I can jump in. It's better to go now
while the smell of your kiss is alive on my lips and echoes
brilliantly in my ears. I have already packed my mouth with
the book of images of your coming and going, of breakfast,
of showers, even that silly one of us folding washed clothes.

Open my coffin: the bitter life of the loveless is chasing me.

Sonnet for My Longed-for Infarction

Why would I suddenly recall the superior vena cava? It's
because my mind is full of my heart, and a doctor is
distracting me with talk of chambers and valves and arteries
that may be blocking. My blood is dressed in purple in my eye,
and is trying to visit my ventricles with gifts of oxygen.

When I open my lids I see his beady machines writing colorful
charts and prescriptions for miracle drugs and waving them
like evidence in court. I feel sorry for him who has never
loved and therefore knows nothing of what breaks a heart.

No, my love, death will not kill me twice as it does cowards
nor will I let the doctor or his modern toys misdiagnose
my malady. I am not ill but loveless; let the infarction rip!

Odd how the mind has a generous chamber for the heart, but
the loving heart thinks not, and to itself is heartless.

Sonnet for My Heart's Failure

My doctor reads a colorful imaging chart and says I
have possible arterial blockage to my heart accounting
for the soft pain in my chest at benign exercise like
racing stairs or like in quiet when I again want her
smile rising over my life like a curtain on an opera.

Fire the machines! It's my lost love that makes my ears
weep at the echoes of her voice. Losing her my heart is
squeezed by her absence, and guilt and anger stick in my
valves and clog my arteries. My blood is dressed in black
and evicted from my veins like an involuntary transfusion.
Widowed, it bleeds internal and builds no one's health.

Doctor, I rejected her and dressed my heart in a vest of
thorns — the heart in love is reason drowned in sweet seas.

I need her to circulate in me, or death, not surgery.

Sonnet for You, My Moon

I want to remove your photograph from the wall where
it watches, kiss it, and weep and weep. While the valley
where I keep my tears is always at flood tide, my eyes
are two meticulous waiters incapable of spilling one drop.

My arm atrophies as it approaches your image and its
haunting smile. My spirit falls into a wide penumbra,
where umbrellas, handkerchiefs, oars and flashlights won't
work and echoes are like ostriches and kiwis who can't soar.

Bells only tinkle for my frayed emotions, afraid to scare
the darkness I wear. I wish I were a jug that could fall and
break, spilling my guts which could be like a creation
myth where I would invent myself again as the better man

sporting your love like a moon in my breast pocket, where it
and my heart would dance, sing, shine, and orbit together.

Sonnet for Me, Your Orbiting Dog

I am a muzzled dog spun by planet you. I can't bite
like I used to. I want to trot in hot chase after you,
not spin in this ellipse with two foci orbiting around
you at this distance with no compensation. I prefer a
section of a parabola as it makes a good antenna for my
erect ears to catch your silent rejections. Pain stuffs
my empty mailbox with the long letters your quiet writes!

Cut my leash. I'm tired of lassoing in the gravity of
your remembered love. Or loosen my muzzle so I can bay
my aria at your smile beating in my heart surrounded by
your loud reticence. Why is it that only your dark side
is turned to me now, when I most need a bone of light?

Please change my bowl of salty tears, or let my voice out
far enough to lick the places where your smile wounds me.

Sonnet for a Child Who Calls

There is a child who calls us each day as I pace the
prison yard of my mistakes. I try to answer but my
mouth is gagged by your silence, my voice is in solitary.

There is a child who calls us each day and its song
enters my ears like glass pins under my fingernails.
The pain is a tunnel where my heart tumbles like a
Mayan falling down the steps of a temple where we left
our footsteps when we visited the *muls* of Yucatan.

I want to offer my beating heart to the child like an
Aztec might, or say "wait" with the volume of truth but
my lips are separated — one sealed in a tomb with my
wishes, the other chained to the wall of your absence.

When the child calls, my emotion stabs me harder, but
the tears of my heart have no key to your barred ears.

Sonnet for the Lovesick Sailor

There is an easily ruptured thread that binds a great love.
Thin, it amplifies in her absence, grows engorged like a
great sail, bends the mast and laughs at the rudder, writes
its own course and ignores the question racing over the sea:

What is navigation without a destination? The lovesick sailor
founders worse than lost, worse than chartless, worse than
sunk or drowned. There is peace in death, and clarity; none in
bobbing, buffeted even by tiny cat's-paws; and prone to
swamping, the sailor bails his tears like a weeping Sisyphus.

Lovewrought, he prays for irrational currents as relief. Moving
is better than not knowing where to move. Purpose tries to comfort
him like a fickle ally, but his heart is a pulsing maelstrom.

Have any sailors survived the shipwreck of "lost in one-way love"?
Yes, but few have learned to splice the elusive thread.

Sonnet Because You Love Me Not

My love does not depend on your loving me though
if you did, as once you did, mine would be sweeter
realized. I loved you before you loved me and after
hard earning your love I threw it away — I know!
But it was yours I threw away, not mine, which I
still hold intact — that's my penitence, my paradox.

It feels like a problem in the carving of wood — I
made a stupid gash in a perfect form, now how can
I correct it? Here the analogy ends, and the irony
begins; the wood is more receptive to my touch,
whereas your voice is steely as the mill saw and
sharply categorical, and now when you relax and laugh

you rip me for that slight lapse, and quickly buzz
my heart with the sharp blade of you love me not.

Sonnet for My Appetite Disorders

How come my bed is empty, even when I am in it?

A box of condoms collecting dust and resentment
on a shelf mocks me, but sex looks like a poison
mushroom to my heartsick libido. I do have an
appetite but it is voracious for the past tense
and even then I can't digest the arrhythmic song
my heart whispers. My spirit is gluttonous for
memories, but no matter how many I serve, it stays
hungry and grows thinner. A smile from you would
be a symphony for my ears, but they have flown so
deep into the woods of silence that I wonder if
they can ever return. None of this looks good to
me and tastes worse, and when I take my eyes to the

window of my reason, there is nothing but blank snow.

Sonnet for the Blackbird of Silence

Not as you left, but once your leaving changed from
a shadow to a stone in my stomach, a beaky blackbird
sat defiantly on my impotent scarecrow shoulder. Yes,
it does remind me of Edgar Allan Poe's raven and his
terrible monologue of "nevermore." Except I am afraid
that this bird wants my vocal chords and so I protect
them by not speaking. Do you remember all the songs I
knew by heart? What if I sing them and the bird eats
them? They are pointless as unsaid prayers, and what
good are they in a box without ears? This blackbird of
silence is your absence I know. It works like a capo
on my throat, but nothing strums my guitar day or night.

I tried sex to break the downward spiral of my spirit
but it was your love my soul hungered for, your love my libido.

Sonnet for My Pawned Heart

When I gave my heart I had no intention of taking it
back. When I tried to take it back, it wouldn't come.

I offered her my net worth — all my love. It was not
enough and late. My heart is hocked and I have no
ticket, and now no one knows what to do. My doctor
tries to find it with machines, but like a quark,
or a black hole, it is only there by inference and
symptoms. She doesn't have it and doesn't care; yet
it exists for me only in her. Too late I realize it
was always in her custody, even during my many doubts.

Now my heart is tiny, and feels tucked in one of three
thimbles. I see it hiding its pain in each, but any
thimble I raise is empty. Oh love, you scalawag hustler,
you pawned my heart, how many tears must I raise to redeem it?

Sonnet for What Ails Me: My Lost Heart

How come you're always with me, but I'm still alone?

My eyes have decided that looking down is enough world
for them because my ears are not invited to the concert
of your hellos, and Love for me is like a don't touch
memory of something I once saw in a museum. My voice
cracks under the weight of so much longing and its
timbre flutters like a flag in an ill wind trying to
pronounce your name. A kiss from you could be salvation,
but your anatomy has no lips for me, and my lips are so
tired of crying that they think death is a party they
should take my heart to. My tears are bored because they
escape so easily from the leaky eyes where I keep them.
As for my lost heart, the posters offering the reward

might as well be blank, because you don't believe you took it.

Sonnet for Love's Only Exit

My heart is a mashed potato in my butterless soul.
It thumps without rhythm or edges, each beat struck
on a flaccid drum. This is the price I pay for my
treason and cowardice - violence against my psyche,
self-hate authorized to govern, masked to scare me.

I never lied when I said I loved you, but my doubt
had racing feet which arrived everywhere before me
and carried a maul to heighten my fear. Now my reason
knows that to love is to enlarge the soul and every
fat atom in it: The box of love has no compartments
no keyhole or handles, and one entrance only — it's
called glory, and one exit only — it's called death.

So my memory lies comfortable with you in my life's
coffin, but without your love my mind buries my body.

Sonnet for My Imprisoned Tears

Solitude knocks at my cell door, seditiously taunting
that tears are only happy when racing barefoot with pain.

Tonight I want to let my tears go free. I want to open
the door of their Alcatraz, give up this job of jailor.
I want to let my tears go free — perhaps downstream
they will irrigate my parched loneliness, or flooding
the flat plain of my noisy silence they will shut it up,
or make a puddle where the moon can visit me at night.

But I buried the map to the dungeon where the sad warden
hides. My tears pace the courtyard of my eyelids meanly
glowering back at me, the stoic armed sentinel watching
the wall for your return with the unsealed pardon love.

Until then, this is my harsh sentence; hard labor for my heart,
solitary for my tears, no parole, no credit for bad time served.

Sonnet for Death the Welcome Trip

When the body is in pain it lies very still afraid
of any motion. Soft medicine scratches the throat
and warm breath feels threatening. But lying still
starts to look like death in state from inside. What
is life but motion, death but perfect stillness?

Yet my pain is afraid of your sound, and even old
echoes hurt me now. Your wide smile would blind my
heart, your voice would open the hydrant of my tears.

But death doesn't frighten me at all, in fact it makes
me laugh. How can fleshless bones caterwauling raise
anything but laughter? I am Mexican in that regard
laughing back at death, all my teeth in full derision.

As every minute of your absence is a massive stone crushing me
death looks amusing: is as welcome as a trip around the world.

Sonnet for Death's Warm Hand

When you left all the lights blew out. In the turbulence
your flight generated I am a sailboat with ripped sheets.
Your gone love is my rudder broke. Your smile packed is
my night star in eternal eclipse. Your singing, once my
charts and instruments, is overboard. Without your mouth
biting, my engine has no throttle. I try to bail your
absence but it swamps my bow: the buoys toll my shipwreck.

No, I don't care if I sink. No fish will eat a man like
me, poisoned by remorse. No shark's tooth could crack the
crust of salt my tears have wrapped me in. Drinking the
whole sea might be enough of an emetic antidote to this
massive overdose of grief I have purposely ingested.

Without your hand to kiss, your smile-light, your breast
to suck, your wool across my face, death's hand feels warm.

Sonnet for Eloping with Death

You loved me, you said, but when I became afraid you
extended your hand not to lead me out of my fear but
to sink a great stake in the center of my heart. That
was not your love that spoke, but your righteous rage.

Yes, I broke sacred promises, but devilish doubt had
ingratiated himself to my love for you, like an Iago
to my Othello. Daily he whispered in my ear, "Your
hair will fall out soon, as will your teeth. And one
morning your staff will be soft never to revive, and
everyone who sees an old man like you, with a young
woman like her, laughs, laughs." Damn guilt got up
eloquent too: "True love is selfless; let her go."

You're gone. Your departure drained my soul. I'm
trading my heart for a hole, and eloping with death.

Sonnet for Death, Kind Aztec

When love is reciprocal nothing is excess. Now
just one of your wry smiles would be an overdose.

My state is a shadow to your love, falling lower
than if attached to your feet. I have a mind but
it's incommunicado. Reason hurts my eyes and sickens
my soul. My spirit generates antibodies to my wit,
and I am a bad pool shot, cueball scratching; a
boxer with open hands. Hope keeps my fading heart
going, but the lab says that your laughter and my
red blood cells eloped, thus my anemia. I had eyes
that read emotions and could parse pain, but they
are water glasses spilling, leaving salt on my psyche.

Man, how many stakes of pain can you drive in your heart?
Death, please, be a kind Aztec and rip my heart out whole.

Sonnet for You Disguised in My Dream

She had a tattoo on her chin of a triangle with the
words Love, Fear, Loss, at each point. Love was in
red, the other two in deep blue and ugly black. When
she wept her right eye launched tears shaped like
cultured pearls, but her left eye cried crucifixes
that crashed and splintered in a pile at her sexy
toes. Nothing about her struck me as strange, and
what I liked best was the part of her that could
sing with her mouth full or closed, and when I bent
and lightly kissed her lips I saw that she was you
turned up out and down at once, and my heart flipped
like a tumbling pigeon fleeing a hawk. Then a Saint
Bernard appeared with a rum keg on his neck and when

I drank, it was your special nectar and I awoke erect.

Sonnet for You about Me

I broke two promises, but they were biologically vital
like breathing and eating. Any other million similarly
shattered would not produce such sharp slivers or pierce
your flesh in so many places. When I woke up from my
nefastus act, my archaeology could not sort and reglue
the shards of our old pot love; my surgery could not
stanch the Saint Sebastian I had carved into your heart.
Now my roaring tsunami of remorse won't even tickle
your hygrometer nor lick your toe. Nothing nuclear I
feel can blast the shield my failure erected around you.

Look, I have become a fool, mewling the same three or
six words; I love you, I am sorry. My eyes are mute:
"Boo hoo" escaped their dictionary. My soul arthritic:

My life extensively defined as pain in every articulation.

Sonnet for So Soon Missing Her

It was only a few hours since she had gone but the space
she left was large and gritty and I entered my bedroom
sniffing for her trace. My nose expected her Opium but
found tobacco instead which on her tee shirt smelled good.

The room still sparkled from the echo of her soft gasping
and I saw that she had left her jeans spread on my bed but
my nose didn't find her in the crotch, and I longed to rub
the lantern that would materialize her. My mind read random
only, leapt to when my mouth was introduced to her breast
and became speechless. My lips improvised, asking my teeth
and tongue to assist the kiss hello. Facing the feast they
salivated in unison, found mound and summit seasoned with

sweat and salt and wasn't that warm milky honey I avidly
drank from the steaming geography of her womanly spout?

Sonnet for You, Songbird

Unlike so many wee songbirds that flee from me you
happily sit on my lap and sigh, sing, coo and whistle
too. My mouth wants to sing you a special man's song,
but my lips, tongue, teeth are muted in your curled
feathers and I drool but still hit that high C over D,
or whatever it is that sopranos or baritones shoot for.

My fingers are less secure, worry to pet you, tinkle
down your spine trying to be the wind, or run across
your abdomen skating like a daddy longlegs over water.

Oh bird, what a symphony of tremors is your rhythm,
what an avalanche of snow your throat loosens, what a
houseful of company is your small visit, what a long
night of dreaming is your sight, what a deep pool for
swimming are your eyes, what a vacuum is your parting.

Sonnet Explaining My Periodic Silences
on the Phone

My hand is empty of your hand. Without you near my voice
wants to sit under a shady tree and suck its thumb. That
part of me that only speaks to me says I should dial you,
make small talk, but in the middle of a phrase I realize

that what I want is you fully over me vertical making me
a man; want my mouth drinking from your hot equator, where
all my tropical storms originate; want your tremors ringing
my ears; want you making my body gag and spit with pleasure.

My impudent nose says to hell with phones, I want her neck,
her hair to smell, her underarms, her raw anatomy. My lips
say they want to kiss your knee, my tongue wants to run mad
painting everything from your ankle to your fertile lawn.

Impolite sex won't stand on line, jumps ahead, stiffens up,
my lips go primitive, recall only sucking and satisfaction.

Portraits

Sonnet for Willie Classen, Middleweight

Who killed Willie Classen? Was it who you, or who me?
Was it colorful gloves camouflaging the hard hands
Macerating his brain as if it were cheap steak, or
Tenderizing mallets fluffing up a fleshy pillow?

Or was it the unsaddled Heroin parading *Paso Fino*
Through the tropical sluiceways of his veins?
Or was it those American Dreams spinning airborne
Like pizzas in his manager's hungry imagination?

Or was it Doctor Left and Doctor Two who could not tell
The dead from the box office? Or the impartial referee,
Eyes in his pockets, who could not hear the tolling bell
Sounding the transubstantiation of Willie Classen?

The ritual heart eaters gathered in the Square Garden
Angrily scream: Vicious cockfights prohibited!

Sonnet for Angelo Monterosa

Monterosa, your body is dead on Avenue A. Angelo,
They found you eyes open staring at the beer
Soaked floorboards. Did you want that? Did
You mind them filling your back with buckshot?

Angelo, I am angry with them all, and you Monterosa
Killed and killers, killing and dealing dope. No good
You were, no good they are. Still, I wish their fate
To be bodies stacking under the same blue smoke.

Monterosa, there is blood on your song, blood on the juke
Box. The cowbell, the conga, and your corpse form the trio
That is the rhinestone pin of my failure, your failure,
Our failure, who loved, but did not rescue Angelo.

Angel, hold him, while I bury him in these clean words,
And pray to see the resurrection of the rose mountain.

Sonnet for Henry Ramos

Henry, your figure flashes in the frame of my eye. Angry
At successive invasions against you, a Puerto Rican hill-
Billy in an Orchard Street suit, you roll the racing form,
Metronoming the thoroughbred horses as they race pounding
The turf with the same rhythm as your insistent litany:

"Daily they insult my kids, my wife, my values, with cold
Stares, cold water and cold radiators; immigrants like me but
They forget, and array against me American axioms like
Get an education, be industrious, learn to speak English."

Your black mustache underlined your rising righteousness
But the roulette ball bounced in the slot that pays in
Bullets, and your contradiction was that you were

Right in your aggression and writs of mandamus
But too American to resist the long-shot, Ramos

Sonnet for Maddog

Maddog Arnold is a friend of mine. Nine
Teen, burdened by murder and homicide
Assault simple and aggravated, arrested
Resisting and disturbing the peace.

"I ain't killed nobody, stabbed nobody, done
Nothing simple, ain't aggravated anybody a'tall
Arkansas, Chicago, the Lower East Side
Them places and racists give me *no* peace."

As he recounts the many multiplying stones
Fast piling across the opening of his life
I hear Handel's Hallelujah chorus
And see the awe-filled audience rise.

Now as Maddog tallies up his trials for me
I stand up.

Sonnet for Joe Stella

Acrid wood smoke reminds me that the last time I saw Joe Stella
He was drinking cheap wine and staring at lazy flames in a barrel.

We lived in tenements that had flues for coal fires but sealed
Or not my mother distrusted them because a great snake had been
Found living in a wall on 114th Street and Madison Avenue
Around the corner from the poolroom where everyone played with
Volatile drugs that also squeezed, bit, ignited and burned.

Something is always burning in Manhattan, and Fat Junior, who
Grew up to be Joe Stella, fired me up because he wouldn't pay
Me back the money I loaned him for bail. Joe shoplifted and
Worked for the animal society picking up stray dogs and using
Dope, and when he had hepatitis I visited him in the hospital
And he swore up and down that he could cool drugs any anytime

but they extinguished him.

Sonnet for Eloy Blanco, Painter
Born 1933, Aguadilla, P.R., Died 1985, N.Y.C.

Eloy Blanco didn't want to come to America, didn't want to
Leave Puerto Rico, didn't want to speak English. It hurt,
So he wouldn't speak English, stammered in Spanish, and
Finally just shut up. When an immigrant child shuts up

State licensed Psychosadists rush to his rescue. Pretending
To understand the chrysalis of silence they unrelentingly
Crush it in their machines. The deranged doctors declared
Eloy Blanco hostile. Reasoning that anyone who resists America

Is clearly insane, they recommended immediate electrocution.
The Law allowed them to plug his brain into a socket and
Make him shake hands with the third rail, introducing high
Voltage to his delicate celestial generator. Eloy Blanco

Rose from the migration, spoke little and seldom smiled;
Painted portraits of others with burned out armatures.

Sonnet for García, Clothes Rack Pusher

Look at García pushing his primitive hand truck hard
In the truth of the garment district and its 8th Avenue
Dreaming of wealth through work and retirement on Social
Security as he pauses next to the auto with Sister Irene.

She is also waiting for a green light and her gray eyes
Also dream: of salving García's very red eyes gleaming
Like rich copper veins in the red soil of Puerto Rico.
García dreams green: plantains, palms, and coconuts and
His green dream is the last stanza of his life's song.

The dresses on his wheeled rack are hung tight as the host
Of numberless Angels crowding the rims of silver chalices
Adorning the gray pupils of Sister Irene's generic basilica.

The lights change. García groans. The vehicles diverge.
García gets no sermon, García gets no heroic couplet.

Sonnet for Raymond Castro

Raymond Castro was good at gin rummy. Always dribbled twice
    before
Taking his right hook shot in the Catholic gym, was handsome like
Alan Ladd, tall and gangly like James Stewart, but did not make
Movies or stutter; sang romantic songs, drank and danced boleros.

Quit Junior High School, took a job packing books at a bindery.
Year after year while I studied or taught Guided Missiles, or
Studied again, Raymond Castro packed books days, drank at night.
Fridays paid last week's bill, Saturdays started credit again.

When asked for a cigarette, he would touch each butt like a bead
On a rosary, reciting, "this one for lunch, these two for dinner,"
Through the pack. When Raymond Castro first got tubercular he
Looked fat as if filled with air, and when he died I don't know
Where I was or where he lies, and the dictionary he gave me signed
"To Jackie, Your Ace, Ray 1952" is misplaced but not forgotten.

Sonnet with Twice the Lines

So afraid! Of him and his gruff hulk and hearing his
huh, huh, huh, husky sound which was all he needed
to terrorize me. Just seeing him grunting toward me
started me trembling. So afraid that I wouldn't go
out to play in front of my stoop, or, asked to go to
the store, I'd scrutinize the sidewalks from my window
before saying yes. So afraid: Of the mute boy, and
his defiant deafness ignoring my "uncle" or "I quit!"

Not even from across the street could I surrender.
He had the far pounding greeting for my jumbo fear
which he could smell from miles away according to my
father who said, it was "due to God who gave each boy
one, at least one, very good thing no matter how
many others he withheld." That was meant to comfort
me, but how? Where could I hide my stinky sweating
from this archenemy, my Dr. Sivana, my Kryptonite?

So afraid that one day my fear got so scared it acted
without me, crossed to the bully and punched him in
the nose and stomach and kicked him twice in the balls
and he let out a new sound which was "whuuuff" and he
suddenly wanted to give up. But I was quaking crying
crazy and his white flag looked red as I was erasing
his sense of smell with a hurricane of howling fingers
furious and frantic, pummeling his nose flat flat flat.

He is in my eye now, and I remember the brilliant fear
so afraid that whoever stole his voice might shut mine.

So. Afraid, he muted me by forcing me to speak in rage;
now I'm sorry that I could not share my voice with him.

Soneto para Manuel de Dios Unanue, Periodista
(Nacido 1943, Cuba, Asesinado 1992, New York City)

Salistes en combate adelantando tu heroísmo con una
Revista que saltaba todas las balas de los bandidos
Que no te pudieron asustar, ni por teléfono, ni por
Correo, y menos por la noche en tus ensueños. Todos
Los vaqueros máximos se quedaron con la quijada caída
Porque no le daba soga fina para amarrarte la lengua
Porque no le daba dinero para atarte por las manos
Porque no te podian quemar con la marca de sus hatos
Porque cuando el cobarde tumbó tu cuerpo del caballo
Nueva York, Cerro Maravilla, Medellin, y Cali y mas
Vieron tu espíritu pararse, escupir, sacudirse el polvo.

Manuel, a quien le legaras tus ojos rayos-x y espuelas?

Manuel, le pedimos al Jefe que regue tinta de tu pluma.

Manuel, damele candela al Diablo — si se deja ver de ti.

Sonnet for Jorge Soto, Painter
Born 1947, New York, Died 1987, Vermont.

Jorge Soto had a brain like Einstein and the body of a bear
With the doubly large attendant appetites. His brain liked
To eat art history, theories of composition, color, line and
Perspective. His brain liked to wrestle with professors and
Curators. His body liked to eat cuchifritos rice beans roast
Pork and tostones. His body liked to drink beer wine whiskey
And heroin. His brain liked visiting museums and art openings,
His body liked women, salsa and soft-lit shooting galleries.

Jorge Soto had a rapidograph for a sixth finger directly
Connected to his brain. Standing or sitting Jorge listened to
his brain by sketching, and when that galloping brain hit the
Speed of light, then Jorge the bear would bend it by rapidly
Injecting a dose of time now into its path. When I am asked,

"Did he make masterpieces?" I say, "Yes, he did, and, he *was* one."

Sonnet for the Cowbell Clapper

The back of his left hand is leaning on the steering
wheel while his palm holds a cowbell without a clapper.
His right wrist whips a fat stick striking the bell
and he is both driving and percussing on 14th Street
at 9 a.m. on this last Thursday of June salsa morning.
The sun is already hot, and his old car may have no air
conditioning but his window is open to share his glee
which pulses to greet me where I stand at a red light.

I watch the car racing in its mad musical wake and I
think of a steam engine and its train whistle blast
behind the billowing smoke. If that was an icon of
the culture of the old West, the lovely lonely hoot
in the open spaces, this is an icon for our new city:

A musical Puerto Rican carboy who is the cowbell's clapper.

Sonnet: Self-Portrait for Yolanda Rodríguez

It broke in eight directions like billiard balls anxious
to find a pocket but I was rubber rails and the solitude
caromed. You were absent and I fit in the hole you left
which went on like a flat eternity and weighed too much.

An ambitious azalea asked for a transfer from the deep
shadow that was my only garden. I tried to answer but
Solitude stole the words from my larynx and demanded a
ransom of precious ingots made from your smile. Then

I tried to copy cowering words hidden in my heart and
Solitude laughed out loud, grabbed my writing hand and
kicked over the inkwell where I kept my tears. Death
came mocking me rattling bones; put his naked toe in
my nitrogen sadness; hissed hysterically with icy tongue:

"You died when you turned her down, now toll your own bell!"

Sonnet for Clemente Soto Vélez, Poet & Patriot
Born 1905, Lares, P.R., Died 1993, Santurce, P.R.

He was so tall that he towered over himself, and his mouth
Was so big that he spat whole Spanish dictionaries freshly
Respelled. He was big enough to call Albizu his better, and
His voice was so grand that when he sang "Yankee, Go Home"
America heard "seditious conspiracy." And when he waved his
Thin finger in the air, it scared Uncle Sam because it wrote
"Armed insurrection." He was so big that he located himself
In the whole world from a window in Lares, Puerto Rico. And

When he finally sent his body where it had to go, he was kind
Enough to stay with his *Wooden Horse* and in *The Promised Land*.
They alone are worth a large fortune, but he's also found in
Trees and in *Internal Embrace*. Whenever you want to hear or
Meet him now, look there and in *The Barren Land*, and wherever
The simplest and smallest Puerto Rican yearns for independence.

Sonnet: Portrait of What's Next

I have come to look upon death without dread or loathing.
Death is what I must do next as unprepared as I did life.
Was I somewhere once fearing the state of life because I
had never been there before and could not find a guide?

Will death absorb me so I will forget my children or Y.R.?
When death itself is fast ending, what might be next?
When death is dying will I be wishing to prolong death,
praying for postponements, aware I am the celebration?

Will I ruminate about the good old early days of death
and miss the first dead friends I made, and musing say,
"He deathed badly, she deathed a good death," and sadly
note that some never had a chance to enjoy their death?

That's what's next: living the madness of life, looking
ahead to living the fates, follies, and mysteries of death!

Sonnet: My Speech to Death

Death, when you call I'm going to walk up fast,
put my hand on your cold clavicle and say this:

"What took you so long? I've been seeing your
hand everywhere since I was born, and I have
been looking forward to your acquaintance from
the time I realized that every moment of living
was a moment of dying. Tell me, Death, are you
another glorious confusion like life? You have
to be better than some of my dark episodes, and I
imagine you as a beautifully photographed quiet
film in artful black and white. Forgive me for
being so chatty — I'm not nervous — it's just
that I know you have endless silence in store

for me, and plenty of time to change my composition."

Sonnet: Portrait as a Dry Thespian

Why are my tears ashamed to cry? Saved tears gain no
interest but cause inflation and irregular cardiac
rates. Spent tears are where the profit is; through
weeping the treasure grows. Yes, the mind has a veto
over tears but cannot legislate arrhythmia. The mind
can obtain injunctions to dam the eyes, but it's the
voice that gets gagged. My tears have wooden stakes
in their hearts, dead Draculas while my heart is a
suicidal necrophiliac cutting off his own oxygen.

My tragedy rages in a sunk volcano, while my tranquil
facade is like a cheap costume. Pained dialogue is in
asides that only stethoscopes and cardiograms record.

Will the lovesick hero win, weep, and save his soul, or
will he lose, curtain falling before his wet aria erupts?

Sonnet for My Conspiring Tears

Why are my tears so shy that they hide behind my eyes?

I tell them it's healthy to run and play but they are
afraid that if they start they won't be stopped and I
will drown in their lagoon. I tell them, "Who cares?
I'm naught now without her company." I try to provoke
them by staring at your photograph each night and I
try to tell it what I feel — that I appear tranquil
because I am hollow inside. I plead for them to bury
my body since my soul long ago split. I say "Tears,
fill up the room so I can be like a sailor buried at
sea, in my own salty brine," but they only huddle tighter
together, and I shake like a yellow leaf that won't fall.

I want to cry and drop dead, since I can't have what I love,
but my tears and death conspire to let me wither on the vine.

Sonnet Substantially like the Words of
Fulano Rodríguez One Position Ahead of Me
on the Unemployment Line

It happens to me all the time/business
Goes up and down but I'm the yo-yo spun
Into the high speed trick called sleeping
Such as I am fast standing in this line now.

Maybe I am also a top, they too sleep
While standing, tightly twirling in place.
I wish I could step out and listen for
The sort of music that I must make.

But this is where the state celebrates its sport.
From cushioned chairs the agents turn your ample
Time against you through a box of lines.
Your string is both your leash and lash.

The faster you spin, the stiller you look.
There's something to learn in that, but what?

Sonnet: Portrait of Me, Biology Alone

I meet biology's five criteria for life, but I am not alive.

My mind, misled by fear's logic, did not listen to my spirit
speak. My blood confessed that you were its red cells and
white, and that your touch kept my systolic pressure up.
My heart stuttered that you are the pendulum that regulates
his beat. My lungs sighed that of air you are that better
part named oxygen. My stomach, categorical, said you are
all of appetite. My racy taste buds said your labia were
nectar on their lips. My eyes, wrung dry like washcloths
explained that you were their chromatic guide. My X-rated
part piped up too; swore your body towering over mine was
what generated sperm, and my shy testicles testified with
images of dessication. My ears missed our singing in bed.

My law of science is irrevocable; without you I am biology alone.

Sonnet: Portrait as a Happy Masochist

Why is forgiveness a rock in you that can't be moved?
Why has my diamond-edged love become so dull it can't
scratch glass, or chip your ceramic rejection? Why has
my voice leapt to a shrill frequency where only my dog
ear can hear it? Why is it that no tear, no matter how
small, tender or perfectly formed, impresses you, while
ordinary ones submerge me? Why is it that whatever song
I sing is flat, and when I swell with longing you only
hear the echo of my self-knowledge bobbing on your oceanic
disappointment. Why won't my pen let my hand stop crying
what reads like invisible ink to you? Can't you toss me
one tiny flower to stem the tidal wave of your absence?

If anguish is my only link to you, then I'm a happily chained
masochist; a little hell from thee is heaven enough for me.

Sonnet for Generous Death

Hitch up your horses, Death, and thanks for this free ride.

I travel light. Unlike Ramses or Amenhotep I have no bags,
no possessions to haul. I won't drag my rice and beans or
green plantains, nor my salsa records. I think Cheops and all
Egyptians were wrong about this luxurious trip's length. I
bet you're quick as Charon and his fleet ferry on the Styx.

I'm no Taíno Cacique, so leave my woman behind. Add ten years
or more to her for these I forfeit. I do want to take my
faithful solitude; for such devotion it deserves to be
buried with me. Don't write anything wry for my epitaph like
"He only understood love after he lost it," but say instead
something positive like "Here lies a fortunate man: Love
slept with him many a night, and then it left him vivid and

turbulent memories to feed him for the rest of his life."

Sonnet: Portrait: Who is That Man
in the Mirror?

Well it ain't the face that launched the thousand ships
but it could topple the towers of Ilium because it looks
so gray. Hadn't he more hair? Teeth that spread in an
Ipana smile? He had nothing but vigor on his heart. This
man worries about fat and weight. Cocktail parties go down
so long like bad old movies. But ain't this the man who sat
with friends discussing their old age? Well then, who
was he, Dorian Grey? And who is this now scowling back?
Didn't he have a black mustache and sparkling eyes? What
are these glasses in two thick prescriptions? Why does
that pinky finger tingle? Why is he always short of
breath and breathing hard? Are those his teeth gone?

How did that imposter robber and his partner Time get
in my mirror; how did they counterfeit my brain and voice?

Sonnet: How Shall I Weep for the Dry-Eyed Me?

Why are my tears so shy? Why do they peek through the
picket fence of my eyelashes, instead of leaping over?
Why are my tears so timid? They won't run the relay
race from my sad heart to my dry eyes, or attempt the
steeplechase leaping over deep pools of memories, and
barriers of big and low self-lies! My lachrymals are
screwed shut tighter than capped fire hydrants in a
summer drought. My weak heart listens to no advice or
news, and reads no poetry. His whole vocabulary is but
irregular sighs, and he pumps more sadness than blood.
Oxygen is no stimulant, and he'd rather inject coffee.
I know he is breaking and he wants to cry, but my tears
are grown children who have left home and won't write.

Heart, because my eyes are dry does not mean they do not break.

Sonnet for the Charlatan Time

Time is a sharp broker offering shares in dubious tomorrows.
He imagines forevers, talks futures, proposes perpetuities,
Has an expandable table, displays elastic enticements, like
Sundials, clocks, calendars, and swears by chronologies.

Watch out for the plaid jacket with wide lapels and loud
Stretchable suspenders, fast hands and even faster rap rap:
Like a three-card monte master he will have you believing
That Time is here when it is clearly not, believing that
Time takes back goods when it doesn't have a return window,
And everybody knows that Time won't write anything down.
Remember, only one man tried to wrestle Time hand to hand,
Einstein in math declaring : "Tick does not equal Tock."

Buyer beware! Time has no memory, and exaggerates eternity.
Don't waste precious today banking his uncertain mañanas.

Sonnet: Love & Death, I Am Grown

Death, I am grown so good, so knowing that you are my
only peer, and Love the only mystery. I should have
been forewarned by your symbols. Death, dressed in your
fine bone tuxedo, lipless smile, cavernous eyes where the
teeny world is easily stored, and tranquilly displayed.

Love, look at yourself, infantile in a preposterous pamper
sash, packing a dangerous bow and errant arrows. Love, I
blame you for my immaturity as you are good looks and silly
flirtations, and a bright light with a hair-trigger switch.
You should be a robust bread I could carry across hungry
loveless times such as grip me now — but I have wrecked my
heart — the only pocket for you. Love and Death, I am grown:

Death, you are maligned, charged with wantonness, when it's Love
who's nuts. Death, take my hand, give me quiet, comfort, peace.

Sonnet for My Godmother

Titi, Titi, you always said you were sick and dying.
But your dog Beauty was always pregnant, and the
Hairy Angora cat always kittened, groups of guppies
Leaping like dolphins in the sunlit tank, as if they
Thought they were birds like the plentiful parakeets.

And every Export Soda cracker can, every Bustelo can
Was full of plants, flowers, and wet aromatic earth.
Your address was Dawson Street in the South Bronx
But your home was a garden from Puerto Rico.

Now outrageous embalmer assassins armed with artificial
Paints and powders have killed you, attempting alchemy
To make you look like benign sleep has come to betime you.

Titi, my consolation is the love in life I gave you
Thus, I have no need to weep ... but I do.

Sonnet for Carmen Agüeros Díaz, Seamstress

My mother was good to the machine. She came forty years
After it was carried strapped on the back of immigrant
Tailors, twenty years after it was anchored to the
Kindling wood loft floor, twenty years after the Triangle
Shirtwaist women choked, burned and leapt out of high
Windows into the infamous factory fire, writing history
And a new building and safety code for industrial America.

Good to the eager machine. Bent over one at home at night,
Rode pregnant down dark tunnels in the tired mornings,
Rode squeezed up early elevators, sang to the hungry Singer,
Knew pattern making, piece work, samples, dresses and shirts,
Fed the punc, punc, punc, puncturing needle for thirty years.

Now she bags her spools for the last time, bobbins silver like her
Hair. Her eyesight, and remnants of her soul, not baggable.

Sonnet for Alejandro Román,
Remarkable Rider

My cousin, Alejandro Román, also known as the Cisco Kid, was
Born a movie star cowboy. He had the mustache and the flair,
Knew how to listen to a horse and train it too. But in the
Little town of Quebradillas, Puerto Rico, no one made movies

So he went North to kill Nazis in Normandy and then moved the
Mail at night at the New York Post Office. Days he rode his
Motorcycle to the stable, changed boots, rode English through
Central Park and married as many women as Artie Shaw. Retired

In Puerto Rico he was asked, "What do you ride more, race more,
Love more, bikes or horses?" "Women," he answered, taking no
Sides, but when he died Harleys and Hondas took one side, *Paso
Finos* and Arabians dressed the other, formed a curious cortege
From church to grave. The shy hearse neither cantered nor roared,

And none of us knew which boots Cisco wore for his last ride.

Sonnet: How I Became a Moving Man

My first day on a moving van my so called partners took
Me up the four flights of narrow creaky stairs in a dark
Walk-up tenement on 108th Street near Park Avenue, and
Pointing to an old round washing machine barked, "Take it

Down!" I knelt as in prayer while they tipped the white
Monster onto my back. I grabbed the sharp rim with both
Hands backwards over my shoulders, stood, and staggered,
Found my shaky balance and, sweating tears, "took it down."

On the sidewalk they saw me staring at my red and raw
Palms and asked me, "What are you going to do now, Kid?"
My angry eyes spoke for the blood-soaked hands, but my
Voice rushed out of my mouth solemn like a church bell.

"Go get the refrigerator," I said. "No," they said, "we will
Teach you straps now that you're a man who knows bleeding."

Sonnet for Delgado the Driver

American dollars, nickels and dimes multiply on the meter
The classy Checker is vintage Detroit cruising the streets
Albany's motor vehicle bureau puts plates on the bumpers
And the New York police photograph the driver and stick
Him on the dash with his number as if he was "Wanted."

When I look closely, it is Jorge Delgado the driver, who has
Red and blue fringe tassels around the rims of all the windows.
Behind the back seat he has a hand-embroidered starched doll
Standing next to a coconut palm tree towering over a ceramic
Deep green avocado, all resting on a hand-embroidered doily.
The radio plays WADO, and under a Puerto Rican flag a neat
Handwritten Spanish sign says, "No Smoking Please Today."

Delgado drives fourteen hours day and night in New York City,
    America.
But he is in Puerto Rico all the time.

Sonnet for Miss Beausoleil

Two threatening kids dared me. I loved her but was ten,
So I surely printed, "Miss Beausoleil is a motherfucker."
Right in Spanish Harlem on Lexington Avenue and 106th Street
Right next to the main entrance of PS 107 grammar school.

The same two aspiring Iagos I'm sure squealed on me and
Her face was hard, but her eyes were the Virgen Dolorosa
Which became X-ray hands thoroughly searching my soul
For evidence of perdition, for evidence of redemption.

I dumbly whispered, "I wrote it and spelled it correctly."

The rest is lost except for this: I didn't know her
Name meant Beautiful Sun, nor how to revise my writing;
Repressed what my punishment was, but never forgot her.

I apologize now, Miss Beausoleil, for me and the terrible kids
And assure you, that I don't value pure spelling anymore.